"I" MATTER: 11 KEYS TO EXCELLENCE

Inspirational Journal Guide to Excellence and Success

by

EXCELL LA FAYETTE, JR.

EXCELL LA FAYETTE, JR.

"I" MATTER: 11 KEYS TO EXCELLENCE

THIS JOURNAL BELONGS TO:

NAME

FROM

DATE

EXCELL LA FAYETTE, JR.

"I" MATTER: 11 KEYS TO EXCELLENCE – *Inspirational Journal Guide to Excellence and Success.* Copyright © 2020 by Excell La Fayette, Jr., La Fayette Enterprises, LLC. All rights reserved. Printed in the United States of America. No part of this journal may be reproduced or transmitted in any form or by any means, electronic or mechanical, including photocopying, recording, or by an information storage and retrieval system – except by a reviewer who may quote brief passages in a review to be printed in a magazine or newspaper, and in the case of The Holy Bible's (KJV, NIV and NKJV) brief scripture quotations embodied at the bottom of pages – without permission in writing from the publisher. This journal is ideal for distribution throughout corporations and organizations.

It also makes a great gift. Volume discounts are available.

Published by: La Fayette Enterprises, LLC

P. O. Box 654, Bristow, OK 74010

Website: www.ExcelltoExcellence.com

Library of Congress Control Number: 2020919768

Paperback (English) ISBN: 978-1-7354317-1-0

Editor: Zina Curlee Paige, Zina-PR.com

"I" MATTER: 11 KEYS TO EXCELLENCE

This journal is dedicated to my parents, Excell and Ruby Mae Clement-La Fayette; my paternal grandparents, Walter Reed and Mary Ann La Fayette; maternal grandparents, Russell Harrison Clement, Henry Bennett Shields (step-grandfather), and Glassie Mae Clement-Shields; their fore-parents, and all the elders that led the way for the freedoms we have today.

And "You"

_____

(Insert your name)

Use this journal as a guide to transform your life, and as a gift to help others unleash their thinking, talents, and dreams from within. Be excited, encouraged, and accountable! Do not be a hindrance to your own success. Let your past motivate your future. Do not settle by just existing in this life.

Thank you,

Excell La Fayette, Jr.

AUTHOR | MOTIVATIONAL SPEAKER | LIFE COACH

EXCELL LA FAYETTE, JR.

"I" MATTER: 11 KEYS TO EXCELLENCE

"I" MATTER: 11 KEYS TO EXCELLENCE

LA FAYETTE ENTERPRISES, LLC

PUBLISHER

www.ExcelltoExcellence.com

EXCELL LA FAYETTE, JR.

"I" MATTER: 11 KEYS TO EXCELLENCE

CONTENTS

Introduction   13-14

Purpose to the User: Because "I" Matter

Take these points and unleash the power of your potential.

   Dream and Ambition

   Create Goal(s)

   Prioritize Goal(s)

   Develop Strategy

   Develop A Vision

   Execute Your Vision

   Unleash The power Within "You" for Excellence

Bible Scriptures   14-15

   The Living Word

"I" Matter   15

   What Is Your Why?

   Get Out of Your Box!

Goal Setting, Re-Assessment and Reflection	15
Conclusion	16
Purpose of the Journal: 11 Keys to Enhance Your Thinking	
Big Picture Thinking	17
Focused Thinking	29
Creative Thinking	41
Realistic Thinking	53
Strategic Thinking	65
Possibility Thinking	77
Reflective Thinking	89
Popular Thinking	101
Shared Thinking	113
Unselfish Thinking	125
Bottom Line Thinking	137

"I" MATTER: 11 KEYS TO EXCELLENCE

About the Author   149-150

Excell La Fayette, Jr.

EXCELL LA FAYETTE, JR.

"I" MATTER: 11 KEYS TO EXCELLENCE

INTRODUCTION

The real purpose of this inspirational journal guide is to operate as an instrument for "You" the reader to visualize that "I" Matter. Create a mindset by using these thinking points below, as building blocks to take action to achieve your ultimate dreams and goals.

This inspirational journal guide is about your dreams and the power to make those dreams come true with your participation by:

- Dreaming – dream big and have an ambition to be successful and do great things.
- Creating goal(s) – stay on track to achieve your ultimate dream.
- Prioritizing goal(s) – this takes discipline and removes the distractors.
- Developing strategy – there are steps and processes you use to reach and achieve your goal.

- Developing a vision – dreams enhance your vision to see clearly. When you have a vision, you can operate efficiently to achieve your goal.
- Executing your vision – as in strategy, you have created your goal(s). You must have a process to go through your steps to complete your objective.
- Unleashing the power within "You" for excellence.

BIBLE SCRIPTURES

The repeated Bible scriptures on several pages are there to represent the Bible as the "Living Word." Each time we read a scripture, even though it may be the same words on the page, it resonates something different in our hearts and mind.

Each time you make a journal entry, your heart and mind are waking up the successful person within you, by taking action to reach your highest potential. These scriptures will motivate you to stop using setbacks, failures, and pressures as excuses. Start visualizing them as challenges and opportunities for success. The scripture urges you to stop hiding behind your past, going through everyday motions, and standing on the sidelines, by becoming the man or woman that God has created you to be.

"I" MATTER

What is your why? Get out of your box! You were put on this earth for a purpose. We have so much congestion in our lives and become consumed with things that do not really matter. It keeps us from reaching our full potential, and it clouds our thinking. Because "you" matter, your gift to this earth, to your family, or the human population is to be the best "you." Because "you" matter, everyone has the innate ability to help one another in many areas. Because "you" matter; we all think differently, and some of those thoughts are kept silent. Those silent thoughts could help enhance this world we live in today. Why you matter, is because "you" are important!

GOAL SETTING, RE-ASSESSMENT AND REFLECTON

As you review these *11 Keys to Excellence*, take some time to write your goals, reflect on your goals, and act on successfully completing your goals.

CONCLUSION

Success means something different to everyone. As you complete this journal, you will pen your thoughts and dreams. You must act on those thoughts and dreams to accomplish your desired outcome. Your actions speak louder than words.

It is my desire, that this thinking and journaling process will reveal that "You" matter. Dig deep inside yourself and release these *11 Keys to Enhance Your Thinking*.

Have a successful journey!

"I" MATTER: 11 KEYS TO EXCELLENCE

11 KEYS TO ENHANCE YOUR THINKING

Key # 1

Big Picture THINKING

Big picture thinking is having the ability to visualize broadly, create ideas, solutions and see possibilities to maximize those opportunities.

> John 10:10 (*KJV*) *I am come that they might have life, and that they might have it more abundantly.*

EXCELL LA FAYETTE, JR.

Date____/____/____

BIG PICTURE THINKING

Use this section below to show how you think big! Write down what your typical day looks like, then compare it to what you want it to be.

_____

_____

_____

_____

_____

_____

_____

_____

John 10:10 (*KJV*) *I am come that they might have life, and that they might have it more abundantly.*

"I" MATTER: 11 KEYS TO EXCELLENCE

Date____/____/____

BIG PICTURE THINKING

_____

_____

_____

_____

_____

_____

_____

_____

_____

_____

_____

John 10:10 (*KJV*) *I am come that they might have life, and that they might have it more abundantly.*

EXCELL LA FAYETTE, JR.

Date____/____/____

BIG PICTURE THINKING

What are some of the barriers that prevent your thoughts?

_____

_____

_____

_____

_____

_____

_____

_____

_____

John 10:10 (KJV) I am come that they might have life, and that they might have it more abundantly.

"I" MATTER: 11 KEYS TO EXCELLENCE

Date____/____/____

BIG PICTURE THINKING

_____

_____

_____

_____

_____

_____

_____

_____

_____

_____

_____

John 10:10 (KJV) I am come that they might have life, and that they might have it more abundantly.

EXCELL LA FAYETTE, JR.

Date____/____/____

BIG PICTURE THINKING

How can you think without limits?

_____

_____

_____

_____

_____

_____

_____

_____

_____

John 10:10 (*KJV*) *I am come that they might have life, and that they might have it more abundantly.*

"I" MATTER: 11 KEYS TO EXCELLENCE

Date____/____/____

BIG PICTURE THINKING

_____
_____
_____
_____
_____
_____
_____
_____
_____
_____
_____
_____

John 10:10 (*KJV*) *I am come that they might have life, and that they might have it more abundantly.*

EXCELL LA FAYETTE, JR.

Date____/____/____

BIG PICTURE THINKING

How can you unchain your thoughts and think like a visionary?

_____

_____

_____

_____

_____

_____

_____

_____

_____

John 10:10 (*KJV*) *I am come that they might have life, and that they might have it more abundantly.*

"I" MATTER: 11 KEYS TO EXCELLENCE

Date____/____/____

BIG PICTURE THINKING

_____

_____

_____

_____

_____

_____

_____

_____

_____

_____

_____

John 10:10 (*KJV*) *I am come that they might have life, and that they might have it more abundantly.*

EXCELL LA FAYETTE, JR.

Date____/____/____

BIG PICTURE THINKING

Write down all your goals--long term and short term.

_____

_____

_____

_____

_____

_____

_____

_____

_____

_____

John 10:10 (*KJV*) *I am come that they might have life, and that they might have it more abundantly.*

"I" MATTER: 11 KEYS TO EXCELLENCE

Date____/____/____

BIG PICTURE THINKING

Write and rank your top "Big Picture" thoughts/goals.

_____

_____

_____

_____

_____

_____

_____

_____

_____

_____

John 10:10 (*KJV*) *I am come that they might have life, and that they might have it more abundantly.*

EXCELL LA FAYETTE, JR.

NOTES

"I" MATTER: 11 KEYS TO EXCELLENCE

Key #2

Focused THINKING

Focused thinking is concentrating on a single topic

or task in mind.

James 1:22 (*NKJV*) *But be doers of the word, and not hearers only, deceiving yourselves.*

EXCELL LA FAYETTE, JR.

Date____/____/____

FOCUSED THINKING

Focusing clears your vision/views. Write down five (5) core focuses.

_____

_____

_____

_____

_____

_____

_____

_____

James 1:22 (*NKJV*) *But be doers of the word, and not hearers only, deceiving yourselves.*

"I" MATTER: 11 KEYS TO EXCELLENCE

Date____/____/____

FOCUSED THINKING

Focusing helps you be a doer. What five (5) actions can you take?

_____

_____

_____

_____

_____

_____

_____

_____

_____

James 1:22 (*NKJV*) *But be doers of the word, and not hearers only, deceiving yourselves.*

EXCELL LA FAYETTE, JR.

Date____/____/____

FOCUSED THINKING

Focused actions are money makers. Name a few ways that you can volunteer, donate to a charity of your choice, and increase your social circle.

_____

_____

_____

_____

_____

_____

_____

_____

_____

James 1:22 (*NKJV*) *But be doers of the word, and not hearers only, deceiving yourselves.*

"I" MATTER: 11 KEYS TO EXCELLENCE

Date____/____/____

FOCUSED THINKING

When focused, 100% of tasks are completed. List five (5) tasks completed.

_____

_____

_____

_____

_____

_____

_____

_____

_____

James 1:22 (*NKJV*) *But be doers of the word, and not hearers only, deceiving yourselves.*

EXCELL LA FAYETTE, JR.

Date____/____/____

FOCUSED THINKING

When focused, the real "You" emerges. Name five (5) ways to practice focusing.

_____

_____

_____

_____

_____

_____

_____

_____

_____

_____

James 1:22 (*NKJV*) *But be doers of the word, and not hearers only, deceiving yourselves.*

"I" MATTER: 11 KEYS TO EXCELLENCE

Date____/____/____

FOCUSED THINKING

Focusing eliminates procrastination. Name five (5) time busters and how you can avoid them.

_____

_____

_____

_____

_____

_____

_____

_____

_____

James 1:22 (*NKJV*) *But be doers of the word, and not hearers only, deceiving yourselves.*

EXCELL LA FAYETTE, JR.

Date____/____/____

FOCUSED THINKING

When focusing, what matters the most to you?

_____

_____

_____

_____

_____

_____

_____

_____

_____

_____

James 1:22 (*NKJV*) *But be doers of the word, and not hearers only, deceiving yourselves.*

"I" MATTER: 11 KEYS TO EXCELLENCE

Date____/____/____

FOCUSED THINKING

Determine why focusing is important to you. List five (5) reasons why sometimes you must put yourself first.

_____

_____

_____

_____

_____

_____

_____

_____

James 1:22 (*NKJV*) *But be doers of the word, and not hearers only, deceiving yourselves.*

EXCELL LA FAYETTE, JR.

Date____/____/____

FOCUSED THINKING

_____

_____

_____

_____

_____

_____

_____

_____

_____

_____

_____

James 1:22 (*NKJV*) *But be doers of the word, and not hearers only, deceiving yourselves.*

"I" MATTER: 11 KEYS TO EXCELLENCE

Date____/____/____

FOCUSED THINKING

Write down completed tasks or priorities of this section.

_____

_____

_____

_____

_____

_____

_____

_____

_____

James 1:22 (*NKJV*) *But be doers of the word, and not hearers only, deceiving yourselves.*

EXCELL LA FAYETTE, JR.

NOTES

"I" MATTER: 11 KEYS TO EXCELLENCE

Key # 3

*Creative **THINKING***

Creative thinking is having a fresh perspective and an unconventional solution to solve a problem or address an issue.

Psalm 46:1 (*NKJV*) *God is our refuge and strength, a very present help in trouble.*

EXCELL LA FAYETTE, JR.

Date____/____/____

CREATIVE THINKING

Unleash your creative thought power. Write down something you have done imaginative in a new way.

_____

_____

_____

_____

_____

_____

_____

Psalm 46:1 (*NKJV*) *God is our refuge and strength, a very present help in trouble.*

"I" MATTER: 11 KEYS TO EXCELLENCE

Date____/____/____

CREATIVE THINKING

How can you change the quality of your thinking?

_____

_____

_____

_____

_____

_____

_____

_____

_____

_____

Psalm 46:1 (*NKJV*) *God is our refuge and strength, a very present help in trouble.*

EXCELL LA FAYETTE, JR.

Date____/____/____

CREATIVE THINKING

Do not let fear hinder your creative thinking. List five (5) ways you have conquered your fears, and how you overcame them.

_____

_____

_____

_____

_____

_____

_____

_____

_____

Psalm 46:1 *(NKJV) God is our refuge and strength, a very present help in trouble.*

"I" MATTER: 11 KEYS TO EXCELLENCE

Date____/____/____

CREATIVE THINKING

You have a creative voice inside you. Write down five (5) thoughts.

_____

_____

_____

_____

_____

_____

_____

_____

Psalm 46:1 (*NKJV*) *God is our refuge and strength, a very present help in trouble.*

EXCELL LA FAYETTE, JR.

Date____/____/____

CREATIVE THINKING

_____

_____

_____

_____

_____

_____

_____

_____

_____

_____

Psalm 46:1 (*NKJV*) *God is our refuge and strength, a very present help in trouble.*

"I" MATTER: 11 KEYS TO EXCELLENCE

Date____/____/____

CREATIVE THINKING

No limits! How have you used your imagination to push yourself towards excellence?

_____

_____

_____

_____

_____

_____

_____

_____

_____

_____

Psalm 46:1 (*NKJV*) *God is our refuge and strength, a very present help in trouble.*

EXCELL LA FAYETTE, JR.

Date____/____/____

CREATIVE THINKING

_____

_____

_____

_____

_____

_____

_____

_____

_____

_____

_____

Psalm 46:1 (*NKJV*) *God is our refuge and strength,*
a very present help in trouble.

"I" MATTER: 11 KEYS TO EXCELLENCE

Date____/____/____

CREATIVE THINKING

Describe your most magical moments.

_____

_____

_____

_____

_____

_____

_____

_____

_____

_____

Psalm 46:1 (*NKJV*) *God is our refuge and strength, a very present help in trouble.*

EXCELL LA FAYETTE, JR.

Date____/____/____

CREATIVE THINKING

List your creative thoughts from this section.

_____

_____

_____

_____

_____

_____

_____

_____

_____

_____

Psalm 46:1 (*NKJV*) *God is our refuge and strength,
a very present help in trouble.*

"I" MATTER: 11 KEYS TO EXCELLENCE

Date____/____/____

CREATIVE THINKING

List top motivators, beliefs, and quotes that motivate your thinking.

_____

_____

_____

_____

_____

_____

_____

_____

Psalm 46:1 (*NKJV*) *God is our refuge and strength, a very present help in trouble.*

EXCELL LA FAYETTE, JR.

NOTES

"I" MATTER: 11 KEYS TO EXCELLENCE

Key # 4

Realistic THINKING

Realistic thinking permits adjustments of thoughts and behavior to the demand of the situation.

Philippians 4:4 (*NKJV*) *Rejoice in the Lord always. Again, I will say, rejoice!*

EXCELL LA FAYETTE, JR.

Date____/____/____

REALISTIC THINKING

Be real with yourself. Name five (5) ways that you enjoy inner peace and celebrate yourself.

_____

_____

_____

_____

_____

_____

_____

_____

Philippians 4:4 (*NKJV*) *Rejoice in the Lord always.*
Again, I will say, rejoice!

"I" MATTER: 11 KEYS TO EXCELLENCE

Date____/____/____

REALISTIC THINKING

_____

_____

_____

_____

_____

_____

_____

_____

_____

_____

_____

_____

Philippians 4:4 (*NKJV*) *Rejoice in the Lord always. Again, I will say, rejoice!*

EXCELL LA FAYETTE, JR.

Date____/____/____

REALISTIC THINKING

Be honest with yourself. Write down five (5) self-reminders.

_____

_____

_____

_____

_____

_____

_____

_____

_____

_____

Philippians 4:4 (*NKJV*) *Rejoice in the Lord always. Again, I will say, rejoice!*

"I" MATTER: 11 KEYS TO EXCELLENCE

Date____/____/____

REALISTIC THINKING

_____

_____

_____

_____

_____

_____

_____

_____

_____

_____

_____

**Philippians 4:4 (*NKJV*) *Rejoice in the Lord always.
Again, I will say, rejoice!***

EXCELL LA FAYETTE, JR.

Date____/____/____

REALISTIC THINKING

It is alright to change. Self-talk helps. What are five (5) questions you would ask yourself to create change?

_____

_____

_____

_____

_____

_____

_____

_____

_____

Philippians 4:4 (*NKJV*) *Rejoice in the Lord always. Again, I will say, rejoice!*

"I" MATTER: 11 KEYS TO EXCELLENCE

Date____/____/____

REALISTIC THINKING

Change is inevitable. What has made you anxious or affected your relationships, goals, lifestyle, and job?

_____

_____

_____

_____

_____

_____

_____

_____

Philippians 4:4 (*NKJV*) *Rejoice in the Lord always. Again, I will say, rejoice!*

EXCELL LA FAYETTE, JR.

Date____/____/____

REALISTIC THINKING

_____

_____

_____

_____

_____

_____

_____

_____

_____

_____

Philippians 4:4 (*NKJV*) *Rejoice in the Lord always.*
Again, I will say, rejoice!

"I" MATTER: 11 KEYS TO EXCELLENCE

Date____/____/____

REALISTIC THINKING

Rejoice in being "You." What is your favorite devotional reading or inspirational quote?

_____

_____

_____

_____

_____

_____

_____

_____

Philippians 4:4 (*NKJV*) *Rejoice in the Lord always. Again, I will say, rejoice!*

EXCELL LA FAYETTE, JR.

Date____/____/____

REALISTIC THINKING

Write the top five (5) real things about you.

_____

_____

_____

_____

_____

_____

_____

_____

_____

Philippians 4:4 (*NKJV*) *Rejoice in the Lord always. Again, I will say, rejoice!*

"I" MATTER: 11 KEYS TO EXCELLENCE

Date____/____/____

REALISTIC THINKING

List five (5) key things that will drive you to be successful.

_____

_____

_____

_____

_____

_____

_____

_____

_____

Philippians 4:4 (*NKJV*) *Rejoice in the Lord always. Again, I will say, rejoice!*

EXCELL LA FAYETTE, JR.

NOTES

"I" MATTER: 11 KEYS TO EXCELLENCE

Key # 5

Strategic THINKING

Strategic thinking is one's capacity for thinking systematically, conceptually, creatively, to reach success in the future.

Malachi 3:6 *(NIV) For I am the Lord, I do not change.*

EXCELL LA FAYETTE, JR.

Date____/____/____

STRATEGIC THINKING

Put your energy in the right places. Name five (5) ways that you cope with change.

_____

_____

_____

_____

_____

_____

_____

_____

Malachi 3:6 *(NIV) For I am the Lord, I do not change.*

"I" MATTER: 11 KEYS TO EXCELLENCE

Date____/____/____

STRATEGIC THINKING

_____

_____

_____

_____

_____

_____

_____

_____

_____

_____

_____

Malachi 3:6 *(NIV) For I am the Lord, I do not change.*

EXCELL LA FAYETTE, JR.

Date____/____/____

STRATEGIC THINKING

What are the steps/processes that you will use to complete your goals?

_____

_____

_____

_____

_____

_____

_____

_____

_____

Malachi 3:6 *(NIV) For I am the Lord, I do not change.*

"I" MATTER: 11 KEYS TO EXCELLENCE

Date____/____/____

STRATEGIC THINKING

_____

_____

_____

_____

_____

_____

_____

_____

_____

_____

_____

Malachi 3:6 *(NIV) For I am the Lord, I do not change.*

STRATEGIC THINKING

Date____/____/____

Name five (5) ways you can draw inspiration from God or others to help your thinking.

_____

_____

_____

_____

_____

_____

_____

_____

_____

Malachi 3:6 *(NIV) For I am the Lord, I do not change.*

"I" MATTER: 11 KEYS TO EXCELLENCE

Date____/____/____

STRATEGIC THINKING

How will you plan to expand your thoughts or thinking processes?

_____

_____

_____

_____

_____

_____

_____

_____

_____

Malachi 3:6 *(NIV) For I am the Lord, I do not change.*

EXCELL LA FAYETTE, JR.

Date____/____/____

STRATEGIC THINKING

What are your short-term plans?

_____

_____

_____

_____

_____

_____

_____

_____

_____

_____

Malachi 3:6 *(NIV) For I am the Lord, I do not change.*

"I" MATTER: 11 KEYS TO EXCELLENCE

Date____/____/____

STRATEGIC THINKING

What are your long-term plans?

_____

_____

_____

_____

_____

_____

_____

_____

_____

_____

Malachi 3:6 *(NIV) For I am the Lord, I do not change.*

EXCELL LA FAYETTE, JR.

Date____/____/____

STRATEGIC THINKING

List why you will strategically complete this exercise.

_____

_____

_____

_____

_____

_____

_____

_____

_____

_____

Malachi 3:6 *(NIV) For I am the Lord, I do not change.*

"I" MATTER: 11 KEYS TO EXCELLENCE

Date____/____/____

STRATEGIC THINKING

List 11 reasons why this exercise is important to you.

_____

_____

_____

_____

_____

_____

_____

_____

_____

_____

_____

Malachi 3:6 *(NIV) For I am the Lord, I do not change.*

EXCELL LA FAYETTE, JR.

NOTES

"I" MATTER: 11 KEYS TO EXCELLENCE

Key # 6

Possibility THINKING

Possibility thinking is the willingness to see possibilities everywhere without limitations.

I Chronicles 28:20 *(NIV) Be strong and of good courage and do it; do not fear nor be dismayed, for the Lord God – my God – will be with you.*
He will not leave you nor forsake you.

EXCELL LA FAYETTE, JR.

Date____/____/____

POSSIBILITY THINKING

Be limitless! Do not let others define you. Name five (5) things that you stand for in your life?

_____

_____

_____

_____

_____

_____

_____

I Chronicles 28:20 *(NIV) Be strong and of good courage and do it; do not fear nor be dismayed, for the Lord God – my God – will be with you. He will not leave you nor forsake you.*

"I" MATTER: 11 KEYS TO EXCELLENCE

Date____/____/____

POSSIBILITY THINKING

_____

_____

_____

_____

_____

_____

_____

_____

_____

_____

I Chronicles 28:20 *(NIV) Be strong and of good courage and do it; do not fear nor be dismayed, for the Lord God – my God – will be with you. He will not leave you nor forsake you.*

EXCELL LA FAYETTE, JR.

Date____/____/____

POSSIBILITY THINKING

Describe a fearless moment in your life.

_____

_____

_____

_____

_____

_____

_____

_____

I Chronicles 28:20 *(NIV) Be strong and of good courage and do it; do not fear nor be dismayed, for the Lord God – my God – will be with you. He will not leave you nor forsake you.*

"I" MATTER: 11 KEYS TO EXCELLENCE

Date____/____/____

POSSIBILITY THINKING

Read an uncommon book and give a brief overview.

_____

_____

_____

_____

_____

_____

_____

_____

I Chronicles 28:20 *(NIV) Be strong and of good courage and do it; do not fear nor be dismayed, for the Lord God – my God – will be with you.*
He will not leave you nor forsake you.

EXCELL LA FAYETTE, JR.

Date____/____/____

POSSIBILITY THINKING

_____
_____
_____
_____
_____
_____
_____
_____
_____
_____

I Chronicles 28:20 *(NIV) Be strong and of good courage and do it; do not fear nor be dismayed, for the Lord God – my God – will be with you. He will not leave you nor forsake you.*

"I" MATTER: 11 KEYS TO EXCELLENCE

Date____/____/____

POSSIBILITY THINKING

List five (5) things that you want to gain, i.e. material, educational, and spiritual.

_____

_____

_____

_____

_____

_____

_____

_____

_____

I Chronicles 28:20 (NIV) Be strong and of good courage and do it; do not fear nor be dismayed, for the Lord God – my God – will be with you.
He will not leave you nor forsake you.

EXCELL LA FAYETTE, JR.

Date____/____/____

POSSIBILITY THINKING

_____

_____

_____

_____

_____

_____

_____

_____

_____

I Chronicles 28:20 (NIV) Be strong and of good courage and do it; do not fear nor be dismayed, for the Lord God – my God – will be with you.
He will not leave you nor forsake you.

"I" MATTER: 11 KEYS TO EXCELLENCE

Date____/____/____

POSSIBILITY THINKING

Dare to dream without limits. Name five (5) extraordinary things that you dare to do different and get outside of your box.

_____

_____

_____

_____

_____

_____

_____

I Chronicles 28:20 *(NIV) Be strong and of good courage and do it; do not fear nor be dismayed, for the Lord God – my God – will be with you. He will not leave you nor forsake you.*

EXCELL LA FAYETTE, JR.

Date____/____/____

POSSIBILITY THINKING

Suggest five (5) ways to change your mindset.

_____

_____

_____

_____

_____

_____

_____

_____

I Chronicles 28:20 *(NIV) Be strong and of good courage and do it; do not fear nor be dismayed, for the Lord God – my God – will be with you. He will not leave you nor forsake you.*

"I" MATTER: 11 KEYS TO EXCELLENCE

Date____/____/____

POSSIBILITY THINKING

List 11 things that you thought were impossible.

_____

_____

_____

_____

_____

_____

_____

_____

_____

_____

_____

I Chronicles 28:20 *(NIV) Be strong and of good courage and do it; do not fear nor be dismayed, for the Lord God – my God – will be with you. He will not leave you nor forsake you.*

EXCELL LA FAYETTE, JR.

NOTES

Key # 7

Reflective THINKING

Reflective thinking is actively questioning and careful consideration of a belief, attitude or knowledge that further consideration leads to a conclusion.

2 Corinthian 4:8 (*NKJV*) *We are pressed on every side, yet not crushed; we are perplexed, but not in despair.*

EXCELL LA FAYETTE, JR.

Date____/____/____

REFLECTIVE THINKING

What are you grateful for?

_____

_____

_____

_____

_____

_____

_____

_____

_____

_____

2 Corinthian 4:8 (*NKJV*) *We are pressed on every side, yet not crushed; we are perplexed, but not in despair.*

"I" MATTER: 11 KEYS TO EXCELLENCE

Date____/____/____

REFLECTIVE THINKING

What is your real story?

_____

_____

_____

_____

_____

_____

_____

_____

_____

_____

2 Corinthian 4:8 (*NKJV*) *We are pressed on every side, yet not crushed; we are perplexed, but not in despair.*

EXCELL LA FAYETTE, JR.

Date____/____/____

REFLECTIVE THINKING

Identify your life changing moments.

_____

_____

_____

_____

_____

_____

_____

_____

_____

_____

2 Corinthian 4:8 (*NKJV*) *We are pressed on every side, yet not crushed; we are perplexed, but not in despair.*

"I" MATTER: 11 KEYS TO EXCELLENCE

Date____/____/____

REFLECTIVE THINKING

List five (5) quotes that changed your life or way of thinking.

_____

_____

_____

_____

_____

_____

_____

_____

_____

_____

2 Corinthian 4:8 (*NKJV*) *We are pressed on every side, yet not crushed; we are perplexed, but not in despair.*

EXCELL LA FAYETTE, JR.

Date____/____/____

REFLECTIVE THINKING

---

2 Corinthian 4:8 (*NKJV*) *We are pressed on every side, yet not crushed; we are perplexed, but not in despair.*

"I" MATTER: 11 KEYS TO EXCELLENCE

Date____/____/____

REFLECTIVE THINKING

List 11 people that changed your life.

_____

_____

_____

_____

_____

_____

_____

_____

_____

_____

_____

2 Corinthian 4:8 (*NKJV*) *We are pressed on every side, yet not crushed; we are perplexed, but not in despair.*

EXCELL LA FAYETTE, JR.

Date____/____/____

REFLECTIVE THINKING

_____

_____

_____

_____

_____

_____

_____

_____

_____

_____

2 Corinthian 4:8 (*NKJV*) *We are pressed on every side, yet not crushed; we are perplexed, but not in despair.*

"I" MATTER: 11 KEYS TO EXCELLENCE

Date____/____/____

REFLECTIVE THINKING

List five (5) victories that you accomplished this past week.

_____

_____

_____

_____

_____

_____

_____

_____

_____

_____

2 Corinthian 4:8 (*NKJV*) *We are pressed on every side, yet not crushed; we are perplexed, but not in despair.*

EXCELL LA FAYETTE, JR.

Date____/____/____

REFLECTIVE THINKING

_____
_____
_____
_____
_____
_____
_____
_____
_____
_____

2 Corinthian 4:8 (*NKJV*) *We are pressed on every side, yet not crushed; we are perplexed, but not in despair.*

"I" MATTER: 11 KEYS TO EXCELLENCE

Date____/____/____

REFLECTIVE THINKING

List 11 challenges that you have overcome.

_____

_____

_____

_____

_____

_____

_____

_____

_____

_____

_____

2 Corinthian 4:8 (*NKJV*) *We are pressed on every side, yet not crushed; we are perplexed, but not in despair.*

ExCELL LA FAYETTE, JR.

NOTES

"I" MATTER: 11 KEYS TO EXCELLENCE

Key # 8

Popular THINKING

Popular thinking is basically following the routine that most people are accustomed to, or not thinking at all.

Hebrews 3:13 *(NIV) But exhort one another daily, while it is called "Today" lest any of you be hardened through the deceitfulness of sin.*

Date____/____/____

POPULAR THINKING

Are you a leader or a follower? What have you done above and beyond to add value to the environment that you live in?

_____

_____

_____

_____

_____

_____

_____

_____

Hebrews 3:13 *(NIV) But exhort one another daily, while it is called "Today" lest any of you be hardened through the deceitfulness of sin.*

"I" MATTER: 11 KEYS TO EXCELLENCE

Date____/____/____

POPULAR THINKING

_____

_____

_____

_____

_____

_____

_____

_____

_____

_____

Hebrews 3:13 *(NIV) But exhort one another daily, while it is called "Today" lest any of you be hardened through the deceitfulness of sin.*

EXCELL LA FAYETTE, JR.

Date____/____/____

POPULAR THINKING

Am I easily influenced by others? Name five (5) rewarding things that you can do to take the time by getting to know yourself.

_____

_____

_____

_____

_____

_____

_____

_____

Hebrews 3:13 *(NIV) But exhort one another daily, while it is called "Today" lest any of you be hardened through the deceitfulness of sin.*

"I" MATTER: 11 KEYS TO EXCELLENCE

Date____/____/____

POPULAR THINKING

_____

_____

_____

_____

_____

_____

_____

_____

_____

_____

Hebrews 3:13 *(NIV) But exhort one another daily, while it is called "Today" lest any of you be hardened through the deceitfulness of sin.*

EXCELL LA FAYETTE, JR.

Date____/____/____

POPULAR THINKING

Am I an agent for change? Name five (5) ways to change your thinking.

_____

_____

_____

_____

_____

_____

_____

_____

_____

Hebrews 3:13 *(NIV) But exhort one another daily, while it is called "Today" lest any of you be hardened through the deceitfulness of sin.*

"I" MATTER: 11 KEYS TO EXCELLENCE

Date____/____/____

POPULAR THINKING

_____

_____

_____

_____

_____

_____

_____

_____

_____

_____

_____

_____

Hebrews 3:13 *(NIV) But exhort one another daily, while it is called "Today" lest any of you be hardened through the deceitfulness of sin.*

EXCELL LA FAYETTE, JR.

Date____/____/____

POPULAR THINKING

Do you just follow the crowds? What things have you done mediocre?

_____

_____

_____

_____

_____

_____

_____

_____

Hebrews 3:13 *(NIV) But exhort one another daily, while it is called "Today" lest any of you be hardened through the deceitfulness of sin.*

"I" MATTER: 11 KEYS TO EXCELLENCE

Date____/____/____

POPULAR THINKING

_____

_____

_____

_____

_____

_____

_____

_____

_____

_____

_____

_____

Hebrews 3:13 *(NIV) But exhort one another daily, while it is called "Today" lest any of you be hardened through the deceitfulness of sin.*

EXCELL LA FAYETTE, JR.

Date____/____/____

POPULAR THINKING

List five (5) initiatives that you have followed that went well.

_____

_____

_____

_____

_____

_____

_____

_____

_____

_____

Hebrews 3:13 *(NIV) But exhort one another daily, while it is called "Today" lest any of you be hardened through the deceitfulness of sin.*

"I" MATTER: 11 KEYS TO EXCELLENCE

Date____/____/____

POPULAR THINKING

List five (5) things that you have followed that did not go well.

_____

_____

_____

_____

_____

_____

_____

_____

_____

_____

Hebrews 3:13 *(NIV) But exhort one another daily, while it is called "Today" lest any of you be hardened through the deceitfulness of sin.*

EXCELL LA FAYETTE, JR.

NOTES

"I" MATTER: 11 KEYS TO EXCELLENCE

Key # 9

Shared THINKING

Shared thinking is several individuals working together in an intellectual way to solve a problem.

Philippians 4:11 *(NKJV) Not that I speak in regard to need for I have learned in whatever state I am, to be content.*

EXCELL LA FAYETTE, JR.

Date____/____/____

SHARED THINKING

List five (5) items of the successes in your life from shared thinking.

_____

_____

_____

_____

_____

_____

_____

_____

Philippians 4:11 *(NKJV) Not that I speak in regard to need, for I have learned in whatever state I am, to be content.*

"I" MATTER: 11 KEYS TO EXCELLENCE

Date____/____/____

SHARED THINKING

Now, rank the five (5) successes in your life from shared thinking.

_____

_____

_____

_____

_____

_____

_____

_____

Philippians 4:11 *(NKJV) Not that I speak in regard to need for I have learned in whatever state I am, to be content.*

EXCELL LA FAYETTE, JR.

Date____/____/____

SHARED THINKING

You are in a divine human partnership. How can you allow God's spirit to lead you?

_____

_____

_____

_____

_____

_____

_____

_____

Philippians 4:11 *(NKJV) Not that I speak in regard to need, for I have learned in whatever state I am, to be content.*

"I" MATTER: 11 KEYS TO EXCELLENCE

Date____/____/____

SHARED THINKING

_____

_____

_____

_____

_____

_____

_____

_____

_____

_____

_____

Philippians 4:11 *(NKJV) Not that I speak in regard to need, for I have learned in whatever state I am, to be content.*

EXCELL LA FAYETTE, JR.

Date____/____/____

SHARED THINKING

What is your most treasured possession because of shared thinking?

_____

_____

_____

_____

_____

_____

_____

_____

_____

Philippians 4:11 *(NKJV) Not that I speak in regard to need, for I have learned in whatever state I am, to be content.*

"I" MATTER: 11 KEYS TO EXCELLENCE

Date____/____/____

SHARED THINKING

What is it about shared thinking that brings you joy and excitement?

_____

_____

_____

_____

_____

_____

_____

_____

Philippians 4:11 *(NKJV) Not that I speak in regard to need, for I have learned in whatever state I am, to be content.*

EXCELL LA FAYETTE, JR.

Date____/____/____

SHARED THINKING

_____

_____

_____

_____

_____

_____

_____

_____

_____

_____

Philippians 4:11 *(NKJV) Not that I speak in regard to need, for I have learned in whatever state I am, to be content.*

"I" MATTER: 11 KEYS TO EXCELLENCE

Date____/____/____

SHARED THINKING

Shared thinking brings new perspectives. What have you done to break out of your old thinking?

_____

_____

_____

_____

_____

_____

_____

_____

Philippians 4:11 *(NKJV) Not that I speak in regard to need, for I have learned in whatever state I am, to be content.*

EXCELL LA FAYETTE, JR.

Date____/____/____

SHARED THINKING

Philippians 4:11 *(NKJV) Not that I speak in regard to need, for I have learned in whatever state I am, to be content.*

"I" MATTER: 11 KEYS TO EXCELLENCE

Date____/____/____

SHARED THINKING

_____

_____

_____

_____

_____

_____

_____

_____

_____

_____

_____

Philippians 4:11 *(NKJV) Not that I speak in regard to need, for I have learned in whatever state I am, to be content.*

# EXCELL LA FAYETTE, JR.

NOTES

"I" MATTER: 11 KEYS TO EXCELLENCE

Key # 10

Unselfish THINKING

Unselfish thinking is thinking about what other people want and need instead of thinking about themselves.

Isaiah 40:31 (*KJV*) *But they that wait upon the Lord shall renew their strength; they shall mount up with wings as eagles; they shall run, and not be weary; and they shall walk, and not faint.*

EXCELL LA FAYETTE, JR.

Date____/____/____

UNSELFISH THINKING

Share a time when you were unselfish, and it benefited someone else.

_____

_____

_____

_____

_____

_____

_____

_____

Isaiah 40:31 (*KJV*) *But they that wait upon the Lord shall renew their strength; they shall mount up with wings as eagles; they shall run, and not be weary; and they shall walk, and not faint.*

"I" MATTER: 11 KEYS TO EXCELLENCE

Date____/____/____

UNSELFISH THINKING

Isaiah 40:31 (*KJV*) *But they that wait upon the Lord shall renew their strength; they shall mount up with wings as eagles; they shall run, and not be weary; and they shall walk, and not faint.*

EXCELL LA FAYETTE, JR.

Date____/____/____

UNSELFISH THINKING

List five (5) feelings or emotions you experienced, when you thought and acted unselfishly.

_____

_____

_____

_____

_____

_____

_____

Isaiah 40:31 (*KJV*) *But they that wait upon the Lord shall renew their strength; they shall mount up with wings as eagles; they shall run, and not be weary; and they shall walk, and not faint.*

"I" MATTER: 11 KEYS TO EXCELLENCE

Date____/____/____

UNSELFISH THINKING

_____

_____

_____

_____

_____

_____

_____

_____

_____

_____

Isaiah 40:31 (*KJV*) *But they that wait upon the Lord shall renew their strength; they shall mount up with wings as eagles; they shall run, and not be weary; and they shall walk, and not faint.*

EXCELL LA FAYETTE, JR.

Date____/____/____

UNSELFISH THINKING

List a quote by an author that keeps you humble.

Isaiah 40:31 (KJV) But they that wait upon the Lord shall renew their strength; they shall mount up with wings as eagles; they shall run, and not be weary; and they shall walk, and not faint.

"I" MATTER: 11 KEYS TO EXCELLENCE

Date____/____/____

UNSELFISH THINKING

What role does spirituality or religion play in your life?

_____

_____

_____

_____

_____

_____

_____

_____

_____

Isaiah 40:31 (*KJV*) *But they that wait upon the Lord shall renew their strength; they shall mount up with wings as eagles; they shall run, and not be weary; and they shall walk, and not faint.*

EXCELL LA FAYETTE, JR.

Date____/____/____

UNSELFISH THINKING

_____

_____

_____

_____

_____

_____

_____

_____

_____

_____

Isaiah 40:31 (*KJV*) *But they that wait upon the Lord shall renew their strength; they shall mount up with wings as eagles; they shall run, and not be weary; and they shall walk, and not faint.*

"I" MATTER: 11 KEYS TO EXCELLENCE

Date____/____/____

UNSELFISH THINKING

List your five (5) most personal acts of unselfishness.

_____

_____

_____

_____

_____

_____

_____

_____

Isaiah 40:31 (*KJV*) *But they that wait upon the Lord shall renew their strength; they shall mount up with wings as eagles; they shall run, and not be weary; and they shall walk, and not faint.*

EXCELL LA FAYETTE, JR.

Date____/____/____

UNSELFISH THINKING

_____

_____

_____

_____

_____

_____

_____

_____

_____

_____

_____

Isaiah 40:31 (*KJV*) *But they that wait upon the Lord shall renew their strength; they shall mount up with wings as eagles; they shall run, and not be weary; and they shall walk, and not faint.*

"I" MATTER: 11 KEYS TO EXCELLENCE

Date____/____/____

UNSELFISH THINKING

List five (5) key events where you were successful at thinking and acting unselfishly.

_____

_____

_____

_____

_____

Isaiah 40:31 (*KJV*) *But they that wait upon the Lord shall renew their strength; they shall mount up with wings as eagles; they shall run, and not be weary; and they shall walk, and not faint.*

EXCELL LA FAYETTE, JR.

NOTES

"I" MATTER: 11 KEYS TO EXCELLENCE

Key # 11

Bottom Line THINKING

Bottom Line thinking is a decision where the most important factor you must consider is what you are willing to accept.

Colossians 3:23 (*KJV*) *And whatsoever ye do, do it heartily, as to the Lord, and not unto men.*

EXCELL LA FAYETTE, JR.

Date____/____/____

BOTTOM LINE THINKING

List five (5) things that helped you in this exercise.

_____

_____

_____

_____

_____

_____

_____

_____

_____

Colossians 3:23 *(KJV) And whatsoever ye do, do it heartily, as to the Lord, and not unto men.*

"I" MATTER: 11 KEYS TO EXCELLENCE

Date____/____/____

BOTTOM LINE THINKING

_____

_____

_____

_____

_____

_____

_____

_____

_____

_____

Colossians 3:23 (*KJV*) *And whatsoever ye do, do it heartily, as to the Lord, and not unto men.*

EXCELL LA FAYETTE, JR.

Date____/____/____

BOTTOM LINE THINKING

List five (5) "Bottom Line" moments that proved successful in your life.

_____

_____

_____

_____

_____

_____

_____

_____

Colossians 3:23 (KJV) And whatsoever ye do, do it heartily, as to the Lord, and not unto men.

"I" MATTER: 11 KEYS TO EXCELLENCE

Date____/____/____

BOTTOM LINE THINKING

_____
_____
_____
_____
_____
_____
_____
_____
_____
_____

Colossians 3:23 (*KJV*) *And whatsoever ye do, do it heartily, as to the Lord, and not unto men.*

EXCELL LA FAYETTE, JR.

Date____/____/____

BOTTOM LINE THINKING

What gives you a sense of purpose?

_____

_____

_____

_____

_____

_____

_____

_____

_____

Colossians 3:23 (*KJV*) *And whatsoever ye do, do it heartily, as to the Lord, and not unto men.*

"I" MATTER: 11 KEYS TO EXCELLENCE

Date____/____/____

BOTTOM LINE THINKING

_____

_____

_____

_____

_____

_____

_____

_____

_____

_____

_____

Colossians 3:23 (*KJV*) *And whatsoever ye do, do it heartily, as to the Lord, and not unto men.*

EXCELL LA FAYETTE, JR.

Date____/____/____

BOTTOM LINE THINKING

How are you handling your work/life balance with a game plan? Name a few.

_____

_____

_____

_____

_____

_____

_____

_____

Colossians 3:23 *(KJV) And whatsoever ye do, do it heartily, as to the Lord, and not unto men.*

"I" MATTER: 11 KEYS TO EXCELLENCE

Date ____/____/____

BOTTOM LINE THINKING

_____

_____

_____

_____

_____

_____

_____

_____

_____

_____

_____

Colossians 3:23 (*KJV*) *And whatsoever ye do, do it heartily, as to the Lord, and not unto men.*

EXCELL LA FAYETTE, JR.

Date____/____/____

BOTTOM LINE THINKING

List five (5) things that you wished you had given more thought to before deciding.

_____

_____

_____

_____

_____

_____

_____

Colossians 3:23 (*KJV*) *And whatsoever ye do, do it heartily, as to the Lord, and not unto men.*

"I" MATTER: 11 KEYS TO EXCELLENCE

Date____/____/____

BOTTOM LINE THINKING

List five (5) events when "Bottom Line" thinking or acting was not made, and what was the outcome?

_____

_____

_____

_____

_____

_____

_____

_____

_____

_____

Colossians 3:23 (*KJV*) *And whatsoever ye do, do it heartily, as to the Lord, and not unto men.*

EXCELL LA FAYETTE, JR.

"I" MATTER: 11 KEYS TO EXCELLENCE

ABOUT THE AUTHOR

Excell La Fayette, Jr. – Referred to by colleagues and industry professionals as the "Billion Dollar Man," and the recipient of the Minority Business News (MBA) Magazine's Billion Dollar Roundtable Award, as Supplier Administration Director of Walmart Stores, Inc., a Fortune 500 Company. During the early stages of Walmart Stores, Inc. supplier diversity initiatives, he led procurement oversight for over $3 Billion, as Supplier Diversity Director. His tenure as a Company Executive lasted over 18 plus years.

As a former Professional Bull Riders (PBR) Stock Contractor (Owner) for nearly five years, he had a prized bull by the name of *"Shaft"* in the PBR Finals for three consecutive years, and two years in the World Finals. His vast knowledge as a specialist in corporate and community relationship building; business consulting; motivational speaking; videography; photography; leading others in their spiritual growth; community leadership, and as a certified professional life coach; all have

EXCELL LA FAYETTE, JR.

demonstrated characteristics of excellence contributing to his success and to the success of others.

Excell is a native of Tulsa, Oklahoma and a graduate of Langston University in Langston, Oklahoma, with a Bachelor of Arts Degree in Broadcast Journalism. He is a graduate of Faith Bible Institute in Monroe, Louisiana, with a Bible College Diploma, and a Certified Professional Life Coach from the International Coach Federation (ICF).

"I" MATTER: 11 KEYS TO EXCELLENCE

NOTES

EXCELL LA FAYETTE, JR.

NOTES

Made in the USA
Monee, IL
01 February 2021